Tantric Sex & Kama Sutra
for Beginners

with
Illustrations

By Alexxa Kline

Introduction

Many relationships become tired and the sex monotonous, you may feel bored and frustrated too. Sound familiar? Need a solution?

For so many of us, the subject of sex and orgasms are taboo. Sex is a natural and beautiful thing which needs celebrating. The Tantra and Kama Sutra teaches us how to do this.

There is a common misconception that the Kama Sutra is merely a sex manual for very bendy people, and that Tantric Sex is for other 'enlightened, spiritual souls and beings' which involves having sex for hours. This is simply not so!

If you want to experience heightened states of sexual pleasure, deep connection with your partner and be at one with the universe, you have come to the right place!

Simply by buying this book, you are already taking your first steps to endless possibilities for an incredible and fulfilling sex life. You have made a conscious decision to explore your sexual self, to rekindle your passion and re-light your fire.

Anyone can enjoy Tantric Sex and Kama Sutra, have incredible orgasms, feel deep connections with their partners and experience intense sexual pleasure, including you!

Many experts and Tantric masters have differing views and teachings on the Tantra. This book is written to give you a beginner understanding with a western approach; sharing ideas to introduce and adapt to your own sexual preferences.

By chance, ten years ago I read an article on Tantric Sex and the Kama Sutra and soon discovered a whole new sexual world awaiting me; the secrets of which I would like to share with you now.

Again, thank you for buying this book, I hope you enjoy it and the profound experiences it will bring.

With Love Alexxa

Copyright 2017 Alexxa Kline - All rights reserved.

This document is geared towards providing exact and reliable information regarding the topic and issue covered. The publication is sold with the idea that the publisher is not required to render accounting, officially permitted, or otherwise, qualified services. If advice is necessary, legal or professional, a practiced individual in the profession should be ordered.

- From a Declaration of Principles which was accepted and approved equally by a Committee of the American Bar Association and a Committee of Publishers and Associations.

In no way is it legal to reproduce, duplicate, or transmit any part of this document in either electronic means or in printed format. Recording of this publication is strictly prohibited and any storage of this document is not allowed unless with written permission from the publisher. All rights reserved.

The information provided herein is stated to be truthful and consistent, in that any liability, in terms of inattention or otherwise, by any usage or abuse of any policies, processes, or directions contained within is the solitary and utter responsibility of the recipient reader. Under no circumstances will any legal responsibility or blame be held against the publisher for any reparation, damages, or monetary loss due to the information herein, either directly or indirectly.

Respective authors own all copyrights not held by the publisher.

The information herein is offered for informational purposes solely, and is universal as so. The presentation of the information is without contract or any type of guarantee assurance.

The trademarks that are used are without any consent, and the publication of the trademark is without permission or backing by the trademark owner. All trademarks and brands within this book are for clarifying purposes only and are the owned by the owners themselves, not affiliated with this document.

Please seek advice and guidance from a professional before embarking on the positions and techniques outlined in this book.

Contents

- Chapter 1 - What is Tantra and Tantric sex?..10
  - What does the word Tantra mean?...11
  - Chapter Tantric Sex – The Basics 12
  - Tantric Sex Myths and Misconceptions 14
  - Tantric Sex - Why So Special? 16
  - Benefits of Tantric Sex 18
  - Problems Tantric sex can overcome 20
  - Men:..20
  - Problems Tantric Sex Can Overcome:...21
  - Women 21
- Chapter 3 Understanding Orgasms..22
- Chapter 4 Tantric Sex – Are you Ready? Is your Partner Ready?............24
- Chapter 5 The ten pledges of Tantric Sex 26
- Chapter 6 Tantric Sex First Steps 28
  - Step 1 Preparation 29
  - Step 2 - Warm Up for Tantric Sex 31
- Chapter 7 Practicing Tantric..33
  - 1 Talk Sex 34
  - 3 Eye gazing 36
  - 4 Harmonizing Breath - yab-yom 37
  - 5 The Arm Wrap...38
  - 6 The Daily Devotion..39
  - 7 Woman-led Valley Exploration 40
  - 8 Worship the Woman - Stri-Puja 41
- Chapter 8 Tantric Top Tips..42

- Chapter 9 Tantric Massage 43
  - A Sexual Tantric Massage Guide 43
  - Massage 1 45
  - The Lingam Massage– For Him 45
  - Tantric Massage 2 48
  - The Yoni Massage for Her 48
- Chapter 10 The Karma Sutra - An Introduction 50
  - What the words mean 50
  - Very Brief History 51
  - Kama Sutra & Common Myths 53
  - The Kama Sutra Sections 54
    - **Section 1 of the Kama Sutra is known as the Introduction** 56
    - **Section 2 of the Kama Sutra is known as the Sexual Union** 57
    - **(Chatus – Shasti)** 57
    - **Section 3 of the Kama Sutra the Acquisition of a Wife** 59
    - **Section 5 of the Kama Sutra is known as Wives of Others** 62
    - **Section 6 of the Kama Sutra is known as Courtesans** .. 62
    - **Section 7 of the Kama Sutra is known as Attraction** 62
- Chapter 11 - Kama Sutra: Are you Ready? Is Your Partner Ready? 63
- Chapter 12 - Understanding Orgasms 64
- Chapter 13 - Kama Sutra Preparation and Next Steps 66
  - Kama Sutra Preparation 66
- Chapter 14 - Kama Sutra Top Tips to Try 69
- Chapter 15 – Foreplay 71
- Chapter 16 - Kama Sutra Kissing Techniques 73

- The Askew Kiss ... 73
- The Bent Kiss ... 74
- The Direct Kiss ... 74
- The Top Kiss ... 74
- The Pressure Kiss ... 74
- The Clip Kiss ... 75
- The Throbbing Kiss ... 75

Chapter 17 - Positions from The Kama Sutra ... 76
- 13 Advanced Sex Positions Illustrated ... 77

15 Kama Sutra Positions Described ... 78
- Kama Sutra Position 1: Widely Opened ... 78
- Kama Sutra Position 2: The Clasping Position ... 79
- Kama Sutra Position 3: The Indrani Position ... 80
- Kama Sutra Position 4: Milk and Water Embrace ... 82
- Kama Sutra Position 5: The Tigress ... 83
- Kama Sutra Position 6: The Congress of the Crow ... 84
- Kama Sutra Position 7: The Lotus ... 85
- Kama Sutra Position 8: Suspended Congress ... 86
- Kama Sutra Position 9: The Splitting of a Bamboo ... 87
- Kama Sutra Position 10: The Pair of Tongs ... 88
- Kama Sutra Position 11 The Dolphin ... 89
- Kama Sutra Position 12: The Curled Angel ... 90
- Kama Sutra Position 13: The Magic Mountain ... 91
- Kama Sutra Position 14: The Afternoon Delight ... 92
- Kama Sutra Position 15: The Glowing Juniper ... 93

Conclusion ... 94

Chapter 1 - What is Tantra and Tantric sex?

The Tantra is a spiritual tradition of which one aspect is to develop and bring about a more refined lovemaking process. Contrary to widespread Western belief, the practice of Tantra is not intended purely for the benefits of enhanced sexual pleasure alone.

Tantra is an ancient text found in Hinduism and Buddhism dating back to the 5th – 9th century CE, making it about 5,000-6,000 years old. The Tantra teaches us to redefine how we think and feel about our body and our desires: that we should not reject, repress, or dismiss these needs but instead embrace and celebrate them.

In Tantra, sexual intercourse is one path to spiritual enlightenment, it is sacred and creates vital Kundalini energy. Kundalini energy is a sexual energy which awakens with the practice e of Tantric sex. This energy will help you and your partner connect to each other and the universe, bringing about enlightened and heightened sexual experiences.

What does the word Tantra mean?

Tantra, often misunderstood in the West comes from ancient Sanskrit, a language from India written many years ago. Today it is still one of the 22 official languages of India.

Sanskrit means 'consecrated' and Sanctified' and is mainly used for religious purposes in Hindu religious festivals and often used in mantras.

Tantra is a key to transformation and connects you to a higher self-awareness, transforming you into the person you are meant to be.

Simply the word Tantra means to weave, to expand and become aware.

Certain practices are used in Tantra and include movement, sounds, and offerings which increase sexual energy.

Practicing Tantra is a way to help heal us, it brings us into the moment and alleviates past hurts and future concerns.

Chapter Tantric Sex – The Basics

It is a common belief that when we participate in sexual intercourse, the main aim is the outcome i.e. to get aroused, to have sex, to orgasm, usually happening quickly or within a relatively short space of time. The result is usually one of tension release, you feel pleasure but it is over quickly, and you are unlikely to have engaged in any of the spiritual aspects of sexual intercourse.

Tantra teaches us to withhold orgasm, particularly ejaculation, so the sexual energy is cultivated and grows. This energy is known as Kundalini and transforms sexual energy into something that is magical, sacred and healing; it brings you to a new level of awareness and enlightenment.

In the United States, Tantra and Tantric Sex are becoming more popular as more and more people learn about it and start to understand the positive and beneficial aspects the practice brings them.

Tantra challenges and rejects the notion that we should repress our basic needs or our earthly desires but instead embrace and honor them.

By the weaving together of the male and the female, we become whole, harmoniously and universally connected to each other.

The male aspect in Tantra is Shiva, the Hindu God, and the female aspect Shakita, the female goddess.

Tantric Sex Myths and Misconceptions

Our knowledge of Tantric sex in the west is limited. There are a couple of examples people think of when mentioning Tantric Sex. The most two common being 'Sting' and the scene from sex in the city where Samantha refuses to have an orgasm!

Tantric sex is not something you have to do for hours on end, it is a slower love making technique so will take more time, but it is not necessary to embark on lovemaking marathons!

It's not all about sex either; Tantric sex doesn't have to include the genitals so is an excellent practice for those who want to be close but don't want to have sexual contact and also for those who have problems with erections and penetration. Tantric sex is about energy and connection, full sexual intercourse will heighten this but only when you are ready.

To enjoy the practice of Tantric sex couples do not have to adopt Tantra doctrines or beliefs or become, yogis, masters or experts in Tantra.

Anyone can practice Tantric sex regardless, all that is required is an open mind and a conscious decision to transform your attitude toward the physical act of sex.

Tantric sex is not just for heterosexuals; it can be adapted, personalized and enjoyed by gay and lesbian couples.

Tantric sex does not lead to sex addiction, affairs or orgies, it is about a loving, spiritual, sexual relationship with your partner.

Tanta is not a religion or a cult or faction; Tantra is a series of practices for you to adapt or adopt as you choose.

Tantric Sex - Why So Special?

You might be wondering what makes Tantric sex so special and what the difference between Tantric sex and what we in the West consider 'ordinary' sex.

Tantric sex emphasizes the importance of connection and pleasure; to expand and prolong the experience of sexual intercourse.

The practice of Tantric sex teaches couples to extend the act of sexual intercourse and to make love utilizing sexual energy.

Sexual energy is powerful and potent; it is an essential ingredient to our health and wellbeing. Tantric sex will help you to harness this power, to weave it, to grow it, to embrace it.

Tantric sex will help you reach a greater and more enhanced form of sexual pleasure and ecstasy. It will take time, practice and a little more effort but it works!

There are also many benefits of trying and practicing Tantric sex. It is great if you want to:

-Try something new

-You want to become more connected and more intimate with your partner

-You want to spice things up and rekindle your passion and relationship

Tantric sex will also:
- Help to heal past hurts
- Deepen your connection to others
- Enrich your world

Benefits of Tantric Sex

Busy lives impact on our sexual desires and interest in sex. Too many of us feel tired and exhausted; we do not pay attention to our own needs and often pay too much attention to the needs of others. Tantric sex helps readdress this imbalance. It reduces negative feelings associated with making time for ourselves; it absolves our sense of guilt and shame allowing us the freedom to enjoy our body and sexual desires.

Tantric sex is a powerful rejuvenator; it will massively improve the sexual health and general health of both partners.

Sex is a stress reliever and natural anti-depressant, learning Tantric sex and how to have frequent orgasms will increase this effect enormously.

Without a doubt and scientifically proven sex and orgasms are one of the best ways to stimulate the production of many chemicals in the brain including serotonin which affects mood. An increase in serotonin lifts low mood and depression. Orgasms also significantly improve the immune system, reducing infections, anxiety, stress and headaches to name but a few.

Will give you a glow and rejuvenate you, ultimately it can make you feel and look younger

Tantric sex will also:

- Improve self-esteem for both partners

- Help you achieve real satisfaction from sex
- Contribute to reducing and alleviating anxiety, depression, apathy, insomnia
- Prolong sexual intercourse, heightening the experience and after effects

Problems Tantric sex can overcome Men:

Most sexual concerns for man are of a physical nature such as erectile dysfunction, it is important to remember Tantric sex is not just about the act of penetration or ejaculation and this can decrease stress, feelings of being under pressure and sexual anxiety and thus improve sexual performance.

Common problems:
- Inability to become erect
- Inability to maintain an erection
- Poor or weak orgasm
- Premature ejaculation
- Tantric sex helps to:
- Extend the sexual intercourse experience
- Maximise sensation
- Increase self-confidence
- Give Better performance
- Give better satisfaction for both partners
- Improve and maintain good sexual health

Problems Tantric Sex Can Overcome: Women

Most sexual problems women in the west encounter are more to do with the mind and can include issues with feelings including guilt, self-esteem, body image and shame.

Common problems

- Poor sensation
- Painful sex
- Bad sexual experiences
- Loss of interest in sex
- Unable to reach orgasm
- Have weak or poor orgasms
- Weak muscles caused by childbirth
- Health concerns
- Phobias
- Inhibitions

Chapter 3 Understanding Orgasms

For women, the physical effects of having an orgasm include faster heartbeat, heavier, quicker breathing and intense contractions of the genital muscles which create the orgasmic sensations. Women can have more than one orgasm, and Tantric sex can help with this as well as amplify the feeling itself, giving intense pleasure and a much stronger than 'normal' orgasm. Tension and pressure are also released and is good for you mentally, spiritually and physically. Orgasms also boost your immune system and thus reduce chance of infections

For men, orgasms happen when muscles contract which in turn result in ejaculation. Premature ejaculation is a frequent problem for men which Tantric sex will address. After and orgasm a man will not be able to have another orgasm for a while which is why Tantric sex can be a beneficial technique as it prolongs the period before ejaculation.

Tantric orgasms differ to having a regular orgasm, the ordinary orgasm is isolated to areas of the genitals and is over quickly, Tantric orgasms rise through the body giving an experience which involves the mind, body, and the soul and will last much longer too.

The more orgasms you have and the stronger they are, the better for your overall health, you emotional well-being, your happiness and spiritual self. Orgasms release a chemical called oxytocin which is linked to your personality and promotes general wellbeing.

Chapter 4 Tantric Sex – Are you Ready? Is your Partner Ready?

Answer yes or no to the questions below. Doing this will help you to decide if Tantric sex is something you are both are you ready for.

1. Do you want to improve the way you currently have sex and enjoy a deeper more meaningful sexual relationship? Y/N

2. Are you prepared to use your breath and breathing techniques into your sex life? Y/N

3. Would you like to experience stronger, longer and multiple orgasms? Y/N

4. Are you willing to try new ideas and positions even if these seem odd or silly? Y/N

5. Do you believe both partners need to reach orgasm to enjoy sexual pleasure? Y/N

6. Would you like your lovemaking to be slower and take longer so you can savor the moment? Y/N

7. Do you want to have sex with your partner on a high spiritual level? Y/N

8. Do you want to improve your sex life? Y/N

9. Are you willing to commit time and energy to learning the practices of Tantric sex? Y/N

10. Do you have an open mind? Y/N

Count the number of yes answers you have and ask your partner to do the same. If you have more yes answers than no's then you are ready to try the practices of Tantric sex, the more yes answers you have the readier you are!

Next study the following ten pledges of Tantric Sex.

Chapter 5 The ten pledges of Tantric Sex

It's up to you how spiritual you want to get, you do not have to adopt all of them, but you need to have a basic understanding and a general belief in these to better benefit from the practice of Tantric sex.

Now you have decided that Tantric sex is for you there are ten pledges you need to be aware of. Explore these and see which feels right for you:

I Pledge:

1. To explore the divinity within me

2. To honor the god and goddess in others

3. To explore my sexuality and sensuality to re-energize and unblock emotions

4. To re-address the balance of my inner self, my relationships and the environment around me

5. To use and share my balance, happiness and spiritual enlightenment for the good of the world

6. To explore and discover my sensuality for the good of my relationships

7. To free myself from past and present emotional obstacle so I can express my spirit and happiness

8. To connect with my inner child for happiness and joy

9. To become a healer and a lover for myself and my partner

10. To be wise and judicious when using my sexual energy, to give me increased pleasure, self-confidence, harmony, balance, and freedom for myself and others

Chapter 6 Tantric Sex First Steps

As we now know Tantric sex isn't all about reaching the orgasm and is not the main purpose of practicing Tantric sex.

Tantric sex is not physically hard to do and is something that can be enjoyed by people of all ages.

It is a slow loving process to savor; not something to accomplish as soon as possible.

Next are some first steps on preparing to practice Tantric sex.

Step 1 Preparation

It is important to prepare for Tantric Sex; Tantric sex isn't something to be rushed and preparation is a key factor.

Make time

Fix a date in your diaries, not only does this help you make sure you make time for yourselves and your relationship it builds anticipation

Create a loving space

It is important to create a loving space. For most people, this will be the bedroom, but it could be anywhere that is safe, that you feel comfortable in and that will offer you privacy.

To help create the room of your choice into a loving space, it will be helpful to do some or all the following:

- Eliminate any annoying distractions

- De-clutter

- Redecorate if necessary

- Enhance the room with flowers, candles, soft furnishings

- Create an ambiance using scent, a powerful element for sensuality (try essential oils such as ylang-ylang or rose)

- Make the space as comfortable as possible, using pillows, blankets, and soft sheets
- Play music quietly that is gentle and mood evoking, make sure it is something that both of you like
- Turn the lights down and shut out the world

Step 2 - Warm Up for Tantric Sex

- Have a candlelit bath together before hand.

- Warm up your body to help move energy, have a good shake of your legs and arms, loosen your shoulders and roll your neck.

- Try to not use the bed, use the floor instead. Using the bed will send signals sleep to your brain, and you want to be alert and enjoy deep connection during your love making

- Make sure you are comfortable, use blankets and duvets and start by lying on the floor with your partner. Take time to touch, caress and stroke each other.

- Use various levels of touching; light stroking, firmer massage, gentle touches. This will awaken your senses and encourage you to take it slow. Remember to build up the anticipation as this will help you manifest sexual energy which is what you are aiming to do.

With practice, you will be in more control of the time it takes to orgasm and orgasms will be far more intense and pleasurable

Don't give up. Tantric sex can take a little while to master, but the result is well worth it. Try to make each sexual interaction last longer than the last. If you do not reach climax it doesn't matter, it is not the main aim of Tantric Sex, and you will have harnessed sexual energy for next time.

Chapter 7 Practicing Tantric

Remember:

- Tantric sex can unlock a more powerful, intense, sexual relationship, leading to heightened pleasure and intense orgasms but is also designed to connect you and your partner together in a more spiritual, universal way – it's not just about the sex!

- Tantric sex can be easily adapted and integrated into our way of life.

- There are many benefits to practicing Tantric sex, both on the physical, spiritual and emotional level.

- Tantric sex is for anyone who wants to make changes in their sexual practices, attitudes, and relationships in a meaningful and respectful way.

- There are many basic Tantric practices you can try to start with.

- Begin with an exercise you feel comfortable doing.

1 Talk Sex

Try to set some time aside with your partner to talk about sex. This can be a general conversation but helpful if you both shared what you enjoy the most and what you enjoy about each the most. Just by talking about sex helps us mentally to think about our sexual selves and can often lead on to sexual unions.

2 The Heart Breath

Practicing the heart breath is a wonderful way to tune into each other. It's also very straightforward and easy to do.

How to do The Heart Breath

Stand to face each other. Look into each other's eyes and place your left hands on your partner's heart. Your partner then places their hand over yours. Try to match each other's breathing for 2 minutes (at least)

3 Eye gazing

This sounds easy but is often tricky to do! If you get the giggles, don't worry! This exercise helps you both to connect and see glimpses of each other's inner core and essence. This practice can be performed on its own or as a starter for a further union. It's great for building trust and good for really seeing each other. Remember eyes are windows to the soul.

How to do Eye Gazing

Sit facing your partner and gaze into one another's eyes. Do this for at least 20 minutes. You can take also join palms. The left palm faces upwards and the right palm down. Try sending energy through the right hands and receive in the left. Doing this will circulate the energy.

4 Harmonizing Breath - yab-yom

Breathing each other's breath is one of the easiest ways to introduce yourselves to the principles of Tantric sex. It is easy to do; it helps you to connect with each other and is known as yab-yom in the Tantra, it is a very connecting, personal, intimate breathing technique. Breath and the act of conscious breathing is a fundamental and important part of Tantra.

How to do The Harmonizing Breath

Sit on your partner's lap (straddle), so you are facing each other. One partner inhales the other exhales. So, you are breathing in and exhaling your partner's breath and vice versa. As your partner breathes out inhale their breath, take the breath down into your body and as you exhale energize the breath with your mind and spirit.

5 The Arm Wrap

This is a really easy technique to do and is a great warm-up exercise. It helps both partners to feel more connected. The skin contact between you will heighten feelings of intimacy and connection.

How to do The Arm Wrap

Sit in you partners lap facing each other. Both wrap your arms around each other tightly and press your bodies against each other.

6 The Daily Devotion

This position is designed to be repeated daily for a week. It builds up sexual energy and is a great practice to harness sexual energy for a union.

The anticipation over the week builds up and will be explosive when the energy is finally released!

How to do The Daily Devotion

In the spoon position, the man places his penis in the woman's vagina every day for a week with no movement for 5-10 minutes. The woman may occasionally squeeze with her vaginal muscles. The man then withdraws his penis. Resist the temptation to have full sexual intercourse. Enjoy the feelings this brings.

7 Woman-led Valley Exploration

This is a prolonged easy practice to try and is a wonderful way for the man to relax and enjoy the pleasure offered by the woman. It enables the man to be less focused on his performance allowing him to benefit from the experience throughout his whole body fully. This also helps slow things down, builds the anticipation, harnesses orgasmic energy, intensifies and heightens the orgasm.

How to do The Woman Led Valley Exploration

This position might be easier to do with the woman on top but can be done in missionary position too. Very slowly the woman will take the man's penis into her vagina. The woman can then play and tease, with very gentle movements, back and forth, circular movements and gentle rising up and down. The man can fully enjoy the sensations which will soon rise and fill the body. The man does nothing apart from receiving the pleasures from the woman.

8 Worship the Woman - Stri-Puja

Stri – Puja means worship of the woman. this is a really good ritual for those who have fewer inhibitions and like to try something different. It is effortless to do and anyone can do it but may take a bit of courage to do it. It is about offering pleasure to the woman, the 'goddess' and is performed by the man.

How to do Stri – Putja

The man creates a setting which includes an altar, using candles, incense, oils, flowers, food, treats, delicacies or other sacred symbols.

Using the sacred symbols, the man has chosen, he offers these to the woman. The man, for example, will feed the woman her food, stroke her body with flowers, silks or other offerings, the man will massage the woman with oils, will kneel, praise and give thanks to her.

The man will then offer to pleasure the woman, the idea of this practice is to become at ease with giving and receiving, to appreciate and adore. It invokes gratitude and opens the door for positive emotions to harmonize.

Chapter 8 Tantric Top Tips

1 Keep Your Eyes Open

Making love with your eyes open is a tried and tested way to evoke deep intimacy and connection with your partner. For some, this might be harder than others and can be introduced in stages if need be. It is often hard to be seen when we feel at our most vulnerable but being truly aware of the act of love by witnessing it will make the experience far more connecting and transformative.

2 Make Love Slowly

Agree in advance that you will make love slowly. The journey is more important than the destination here. Spend time arousing each other; foreplay is essential here. The longer you take stimulating each other, the more sexual energy will build. Pause if you need. Use the time to fully connect to each other, enjoying the moment and allowing yourself to linger there. Breath slowly, concentrating on your breath. Consciously postpone the point of reaching orgasm. When you do reach orgasm, you will find it is a much more intense and pleasurable experience. Much more stress and tension will be released, and the benefits of this both physically and mentally will last much longer.

3 Breathe slowly before climax

When you feel you might climax and you want to prolong the experience slow down your breathing. Usually, when orgasming, we breathe more quickly, particularly women. If you instead take deep, slow breaths down to your stomach, the orgasm will last much longer and be of greater intensity. You can practice this technique during Tantric and regular sex.

4 Choose the Right Positions

Remember to select positions for sexual intercourse that won't make you reach orgasm too quickly, the slower you go, the more energy there will be, and the ultimate orgasm you and your partner will have will be far more intense and pleasurable.

Final Note on Tantric Sex

Tantric sex is something to be cherished and to be practiced with integrity and kindness.

Chapter 9 Tantric Massage

A Sexual Tantric Massage Guide

In this easy to follow guide, you will find instructions on how to perform two sexual massages, one for him and one for her.

Tantric massages do not necessarily involve the genitals. The two massages in the section however will.

Preparation

*Refer to preparation for Tantric sex and creating a Love Space in section one.

Time to try a Tantric massage?

At an agreed time that works for you both, where you won't be interrupted and can focus on the experience without being disturbed. (involves no sex, this is a massage practice)

Massage 1
The Lingam Massage– For Him

This massage is for the male; however, it doesn't matter if the giver is male or female. Prepare your love space, making it as sensual as possible. Ensure you have oils to hand.

How to do the Lingam Massage

To start the man lies spread eagle on his back. This position encourages trust and can be taken a step further with a blindfold (optional!) the floor is perfect, but if you don't have enough floor space, you can do this on the bed. Place cushions beneath the lower back and under the knees.

Giver: Warm the oil in your hands, gently start to massage the genitals, starting with the testicles. Ensure a light touch as this is a very sensitive area and you want it to be pleasurable, not painful! Avoiding contact with the penis, start to massage outwards towards the inner thighs, the stomach and chest. Take your time and allow your partner to feel and appreciate his senses and your touch.

When you feel ready, focus your attention on the penis. Ensuring your hands are still oiled (use more if necessary) take hold of the penis gently with a light touch, apply a little pressure, so you have a gentle but firm hold of the bottom of the stem (base) of the penis.

Take your other hand with your palm open and gently stroke the penis from the bottom to the top, when you reach the tip change hands and with just a little bit of pressure massage the end of the penis using circular motions. Do this about five times.

Move on to what is known as sweet spots.

Locating the area between the testicles and anus, gently massage using the pad of your finger. You can gently increase pressure, speed, and direction but none of the movements here are to be done too frantically.

Under the testicles there is an area approximately the size of a pea, apply a little pressure. Initially, this may feel a little uncomfortable but can lead to ejaculation. You will need to tune into your partner and be able to tell if he is about to reach orgasm. If so stop. This massage is a perfect way to introduce yourself to Tantric sex.

Receiver:

- Relax and enjoy the experience, feel the love you are receiving.

- Don't think or act, just try and clear your mind.

- Be mindful of your body, focus on the sensations you are feeling.

- Don't try to influence or engineer an outcome, just let it, and yourself be.

- Trust in your partner, feel the sexual energy and merge with it - become it.

Tantric Massage 2
The Yoni Massage for Her

Yoni means the vagina in Sanskrit, so very simply this is a vaginal massage! It is easy to do and will give the woman a lot of pleasure.

The Yoni massage has a healing effect, it raises sexual energy in the vagina and connects the receiver to her vagina physically, emotionally as well as spiritually.

The woman lies on back with a pillow placed under her head, also place pillows under her lower back and knees. Remember the aim is not to orgasm but to encourage connection and pleasure.

How to do the Yoni Massage

Giver: Take a vaginal lip between your index finger and thumb. Gently move your finger and thumb up and down each lip in a gliding motion, taking as much time as possible. When you have done one lip, do the other.

Receiver:

- Relax and enjoy the experience, feel the love you are receiving

- Don't think or act, just try and clear your mind

- Be mindful of your body, focus on the sensations you are feeling

- Don't try to influence or engineer an outcome, just let it and yourself be

- Trust in your partner, feel the sexual energy and merge with it - become it.

I hope that the exercises and guidance on Tantra and Tantric sex in this book will help you to fulfil a more loving, deeper relationship with yourself, your partner and the universe.

Enjoy!

Please seek advice and guidance from a professional before embarking on the positions and techniques outlined in this book.

Chapter 10 The Karma Sutra

An Introduction

This book offers an overview and summary of the Kama Sutra including common myths, the history, philosophy and principles involved. There are illustrations and descriptive positions for you to try.

First, it is important you understand the basics of the Kama Sutra.

What the words mean

Kama: Simply refers to desire, longing, and wishes. It involves all five senses; sight, taste, sound, touch, smell and the pleasures of each

Sutra: In Sanskrit Sutra means a sacred thread or a 'code.' Often Sutra's are used in rituals, meditation, and chants.

Very Brief History

The Kama Sutra is an ancient text which originated in India; it is not clear when but most likely around the 3rd century. It was written by Mallanaga Vatsyayana to help couples enjoy heightened sexual pleasure and to redefine their knowledge, practice, and experience of love and lovemaking through enlightenment.

It encourages partners to experiment with positions other than the traditional missionary position and keeps sexual intercourse fresh, exciting, more intense and pleasurable.

All the positions in the Kama Sutra are designed to not give one partner more pleasure than the other; it is important that both feel the union is equally pleasurable, this is known as samabhog in the Kama Sutra.

A little-known fact: The Kama Sutra is from a larger collection of texts known as the Kama Shastra.

The author of the Kama Sutra is thought to be Vatsyayana who is given credit in nearly every translation. However, it is a common belief that Vatsyayana was more the collector and teacher of wisdom learned over many hundreds of years rather than the author per se.

☐

Kama Sutra & Common Myths

Myth: You need to be super human, extra supple, or a yoga expert to be able to practice positions from the Kama Sutra

Truth: Anyone can practice the Kama Sutra.

Myth: The Kama Sutra is just a sex manual

Truth: The Kama Sutra is about how to enjoy healthy loving relationships using certain techniques and practices, it is so much more than a sex manual.

Myth: The Kama Sutra is about male dominance and male pleasure

Truth: The Kama Sutra requires equal participation, it is not about dominance or passive sex; it is about exploring sex positions that are equally fulfilling for both partners.

You don't have to have a long-term partner, and the Kama Sutra will help you spice up your love life, and sex needs never be boring again!

☐

The Kama Sutra Sections

The Kama Sutra consists of seven sections, with only one (the second) being about sexual union, it is here that details different sexual positions.

The seven chapters of the Kama Sutra are:

1. Introduction
2. Sexual union
3. Acquisition of a Wife
4. Wives and their nature
5. Wives of others
6. Courtesans
7. Attraction

The Kama Sutra, although ancient and translated many times offer's much guidance on how to have a fulfilling relationship and sex life.

In the West, the Kama Sutra has earnt itself a reputation as a sex manual. In the East, it is considered a sacred Sanskrit

To give a broader understanding of the Kama Sutra a summary of the sections or books contained in the whole of the Kama Sutra is next.

Please note when reading that it is only the second section – Sexual Union- which has stood the test of time and is the section we are concentrating on this book.

Section 1 of the Kama Sutra is known as the Introduction

The introduction of the Kama Sutra details a general overview of the principles. It also describes the creation of men and women, the gods involved and rules of which to exist by.

Brahma, is the Lord of beings and the creator of rules which to live by. These are:

Dharma - one's duty during life on earth; the way we live our lives and the responsibilities and standards we must follow. These include specific duties, laws and moral obligations. We need to develop these for the harmony of the universe and cosmic order.

Artha – the accumulation of material wealth includes financial prosperity, how we make a living and gain financial security

Kama – the pleasure of the five senses including our sexual desires. Also, being true to our emotions, passions, our love, and life, at the same time remaining respectful and adhering to the laws of Artha and moral our obligation of Dharma

Section 2 of the Kama Sutra is known as the Sexual Union
(Chatus – Shasti)

The Kama Sutra is for both men and women to study and learn.

There are 64 positions in this section known as Chatus Shasti which are designed specifically to give maximum pleasure and intense sexual stimulation, thus resulting in cosmic orgasm and a state of bliss for both partners.

Divided by gender men and women are given attributions unique to the individual and placed into groups. For males depending on the size of their penis (or lingam in the Kama Sutra) or females the size of their vagina (or yoni in the Kama Sutra).

The categories for the male are:

- The Hare
- The Bull
- The Horse

The categories for the female are:
- The Deer

- The Mare

- The Elephant

In the Kama Sutra, it is the belief that each partner's genitals should match in size, however, in the West, it is not necessary and is impractical and unhelpful to think in this way.

Section 3 of the Kama Sutra the Acquisition of a Wife

This is known as the Acquisition of a Wife and discusses marriage. Due to its approach, it is not very relevant to the western world and western relationships but gives a fascinating insight into how the other sections of the Kama Sutra were applied. The chapter 'Acquisition of a Wife' tells how a man is to match with a virgin. The families of the couple would assist in this, and astrologers would also be consulted to make sure the pairing was good. After the marriage, the man would abstain from making any sexual advances to build up his new wife's confidence for three days. He would further encourage his wife to become more confident for ten days making advances until trust was sufficient enough for full sexual intercourse to take place at which time the man could assert his dominance.

Section 4 of the Kama Sutra Wives and Their Nature

Is known as Wives and Their Nature

It discusses the female and her role. Again, this chapter is outdated, and the information here is just to offer an insight into the practices of Kama Sutra many years ago. The element of how love develops is an interesting perspective too.

Put very simply here this section describes four types of love:

- Love that forms by habit

- Love by imagination

- Love how imagined by both parties

- Love which is outside the marriage – of the world

The role of the woman is also set out here and involves:

Housework; keeping the home tidy and clean.

Preparing meals and taking great care to incorporate food which her husband likes and that is good for him.

The man can remarry if the wife has an ill temper or if she is not loved by the husband also if she cannot have children or has only girls. In this scenario, the man can take a second wife which the first must take care of as if she were her daughter.

Section 5 of the Kama Sutra is known as Wives of Others

This part of the Kama Sutra deals with the nature of men and women and how each respond to advances from the other. It discusses differences in their responses to rejection and offers advice on how the man can seduce and attract the woman of his choice.

Section 6 of the Kama Sutra is known as Courtesans

In the Kama Sutra, the courtesan is needed to make sure men have companions when they need them, to help with confidence and self-esteem to help them pursue a wife.

Section 7 of the Kama Sutra is known as Attraction

This section is about men and women making themselves more attractive including adorning the body using oils, pastes, and ointments, including the decoration of genitals. This chapter also includes recipes for aphrodisiacs, impotence, sexual inabilities and stamina.

Chapter 11 - Kama Sutra: Are you Ready? Is Your Partner Ready?

Answer the questions below, ask your partner to do the same to help you to decide if positions from the Kama Sutra are something you both want to try.

1. Do you want to change the way you currently have sex and enjoy a deeper more meaningful sexual relationship? Y/N

2. Would you like to experience stronger, longer and multiple orgasms? Y/N

3. Are you willing to try ideas and positions even if these seem odd or silly? Y/N

4. Do you want a better sex life? Y/N

5. Do you want to have sex with your partner on a high spiritual level? Y/N

6. Are you willing to commit time and energy to learning the positions in the Kama Sutra? Y/N

7. Do you have an open mind? Y/N

8. Are you reasonably flexible and fit? Y/N

Count the number of yes answers you have and ask your partner to do the same. If you have more yes answers than no's then you are ready to try positions from the Kama Sutra, the more yes answers, the readier you are!

Chapter 12 - Understanding Orgasms

For women, the physical effects of having an orgasm include faster heartbeat, heavier, quicker breathing and intense contractions of the genital muscles which create the orgasmic sensations. Women can have more than one orgasm, and positions from the Kama Sutra can help with this as well as amplify the feeling itself, giving intense pleasure and a much stronger than 'normal' orgasm.

Tension and pressure are also released and is good for you mentally, spiritually and physically. Orgasms also boost your immune system and thus reduce chance of infections

For men, orgasms happen when the muscles contract, resulting in ejaculation. Positions from the Kama Sutra can improve a man's sexual performance in many ways, from lasting longer to better technique and enhanced orgasms.

The more orgasms you have and the stronger they are, the better for your overall health, your emotional well-being and your general happiness. Orgasms release a chemical called oxytocin which is linked to your personality and promotes general wellbeing.

Chapter 13 - Kama Sutra Preparation and Next Steps

It is important to make sure both you and your partner are ready to try some new sexual positions. Preparation is the key, and it is important to agree in advance which you will try. The Kama Sutra is something you will need to practice and not take too seriously, especially if things don't go right!

The positions in this book are mostly beginner level with a few more advanced for those who are more flexible and bendy.

Kama Sutra Preparation

Step 1 Make time

Fix a date in your diaries, not only does this help you make sure you make time for yourselves and your relationship it builds anticipation. Together choose a position or a warm up that you feel comfortable trying.

Step 2 Create a loving space

Beneficial for creating the mood, set the scene. For most people, this will be the bedroom, but it could be anywhere that is safe, that you feel comfortable in and that will offer you privacy.

To prepare the room:

- Eliminate any annoying distractions

- De-clutter

- Redecorate if necessary

- Enhance the room with flowers, candles, soft furnishings

- Create an ambiance using scent, a powerful element for sensuality (try essential oils such as ylang-ylang or rose)

- Make the space as comfortable as possible, using pillows, blankets, and soft sheets

- Play music quietly that is gentle and mood evoking, make sure it is something that both of you like

- Turn the lights down and shut out the world

Step 3 Set the Ambience

Have a candle-lit bath together before hand.

Warm up your body to help move energy, have a good shake of your legs and arms, loosen your shoulders and roll your neck.

Chapter 14 - Kama Sutra Top Tips to Try

1 Keep Your Eyes Open

Making love with your eyes open is a tried and tested way to evoke deep intimacy and connection with your partner. Some people might find this difficult so introduce in stages if need be. It is often hard to be seen when we feel at our most vulnerable but being aware of the act of love by witnessing it will make the experience far more connecting and transformative.

2 Make Love Slowly

Decide beforehand that you will make love slowly. The journey is more important than the destination here. Spend time arousing each other; foreplay is essential. The longer you take stimulating each other, the more the sexual energy will build. Pause if you need. Use the time to fully connect to each other, enjoying the moment and allowing yourself to linger there. Breath slowly, concentrating on your breath. Consciously postpone the point of reaching orgasm. When you do reach orgasm, you will find it is a much more intense and pleasurable experience. Much more stress and tension will be released, and the benefits of this both physically and mentally will last much longer.

3 Breathe slowly before climax

When you feel you might climax and you want to prolong the experience slow down your breathing. Usually, when orgasming, we breathe more quickly, particularly women. If you instead take deep, slow breaths down to your stomach, the orgasm will last much longer and be of greater intensity.

4 Choose the Right Positions

Remember to choose positions for sexual intercourse that won't make you reach orgasm too quickly, the slower you go, the more energy there will be, and the orgasm you and your partner will have will be far more intense and pleasurable.

Enjoy!

Chapter 15 – Foreplay

Foreplay is a wonderful way to start your lovemaking, building anticipation, increases your sexual appetite and will heighten your senses in any sexual union.

Start your foreplay by kissing and caressing each other. As you are warming up a good technique to try is the 'Eastern Swirl and Poke' kiss. This kiss involves the man using his tongue to swirl around the woman's nipple, of course, this can be done vice versa too. Progress to poking the nipple with the tip of the tongue. This technique can also be used on the genitalia too.

Massaging oil into the breasts is a perfect way to warm up and get you both in the mood.

Grinding is a fantastic way for the woman to stimulate her pubic mound, you can do this with or without your clothes on. The woman rubs and grinds herself against the man's thigh. Doing this can be a great turn on for both and is particularly stimulating for the woman.

Focus on erogenous zones such as the ears, nipping, licking and pulling with your mouth.

The backs of the knees are particularly erogenous too. Try kissing each other here to see what happens.

Kissing the neck, inside of the wrists and fingers is also an excellent way to spice up your foreplay and build anticipation

Use hot and cold to maximize sensations. For example, have an icicle and make your tongue cold, or to give a mind-blowing orgasm try using a hot mouth.

Most of us we become creatures of habit, it is good to get out of you comfort zone and try different things.

Chapter 16 - Kama Sutra Kissing Techniques

There are many reasons why we kiss, and there are many types of kissing. Kissing is a bond forming action between two people. Most of us are familiar with the kiss on the cheek as a welcoming gesture, the air kiss, the kiss on the forehead as an act of affection and so forth. There is also the kissing we share with our partner.

The Kama Sutra places significant importance on the kiss, and there are many different kisses to evoke different emotions and passion. Try kissing more before moving on to sex.

Quite often the act of kissing leads to sexual intercourse and is an indication that we are feeling in need of close physical contact. Most of us become habitual kissers with our partners, we kiss in the same way, using the same kisses. The Kama Sutra offers a whole new perspective to the art of kissing, sharing techniques to keep things passionate and exciting.

Here are some kissing techniques from the Kama Sutra to try:

The Askew Kiss
Key Words: Passion, Intensity

A very simple kiss and one you are probably already familiar with doing. To do this kiss heads are titled which allows the tongue to enter deeply, it is a fantastic kiss to provoke a profound, passionate sexual experience.

The Bent Kiss
Key Words: Romance, Gentle, Tantric

A romantic kissing technique. One will tilt their head back and take the chin of their partner in their hand and then kiss them gently; this is a great kiss for starting slow, it can be used in Tantric sex too and is a real sexual energy builder.

The Direct Kiss
Key Words: Excitement, Foreplay, Passion

The kiss is performed facing each other and involves licking, sucking, flicking of the tongue, it is playful and steamy and is a sign that a very passionate encounter will follow

The Top Kiss
Key Words: Excitement, Sensation, Foreplay

One partner with their teeth pulls and sucks the other partner's top lip; the other partner does the same to the others bottom lip. Alternating this, so it is vice versa with the use of the tongue in between can be a great passion builder and is perfect for foreplay as it excites the senses.

The Pressure Kiss
Key Words: Sensation, Passion

To practice this, the partner must have the mouth closed while the other bites the lips. (More nip than bite – you need to be careful that you don't cause pain!) This kiss can be adapted if you prefer not to bite and instead while one partner remains with lips closed the other kisses using a lot of pressure.

The Clip Kiss
Key Words Teasing, Anticipation

To do this kiss one partner using their tongue to touch and flick and lick the other person's lips and tongue, it is very pleasurable for both.

The Throbbing Kiss
Key Words: Romance, Tenderness, and Love

This kiss involves one partner giving the other lots of small kisses on the mouth.

Chapter 17 - Positions from The Kama Sutra

Once you have warmed up with foreplay, you can move on to trying out some of the positions from the Kama Sutra. With practice, you will be able to master many of these.

There are 64 positions in the Kama Sutra which vary from easy - hard to perform.

Don't be put off if they sound funny or ridiculous – these tried and tested positions are proven to make sexual intercourse more pleasurable and give longer and stronger orgasms.

You may not be able to do them all but you can certainly have fun trying, and practice makes perfect!

Now it's time to explore some of the easier, more commonly practiced of these positions. On the next page are 13 advanced sex positions illustrated and a further 15 described positions from the Kama Sutra to try. (Yay) Enjoy!

13 Advanced Sex Positions Illustrated

15 Kama Sutra Positions Described

Kama Sutra Position 1: Widely Opened

A fantastic position for those new to exploring the Kama Sutra and Kama Sutra positions. Don't let the name put you off; Widely Opened is very sexy and like the standard missionary position but with added spice! It's a good place to start as will be a position you are already familiar doing.

How to Perform Widely Open

- The woman lies on the bed, and the man kneels in front of her.

- Raising her bum, the woman wraps her legs around the man's body.

- The woman arches her back and leans backward as the man holds her under her back.

- The man enters the woman's vagina with his penis and thrusts himself in and out.

Benefits of The Widely Open Position

A flattering position for the woman in, this will arouse the man, and the woman will feel sexy and beautiful.

The man will be able to show off his body strength which can be a real turn-on for both.

Kama Sutra Position 2: The Clasping Position

If you want complete and total physical contact with your partner, try the Clasping position. This position does not require you to be a yoga guru and can be practiced by beginners. It's a wonderful way to introduce yourself to the positions of the Kama Sutra.

How to Perform the Clasping Position

- The man lies down flat on the bed with his legs stretched out in front of him.

- The woman lies on top of him, face to face, chest to chest, hips to hips, allowing the man to enter her.

- As he enters the woman stretches her legs back.

- Once fully penetrated the woman begins to move forwards and backward. Starting slowly then finding the right rhythm for both.

Benefits of The Clasping Position

The Clasping is perfect for being physically close to your partner; it is a tender, gentle position when practiced that is physically very fulfilling and brings about emotional connection too. Traditionally it is done with the man on top, but here it is the woman that will go on top. You can do this side by side too and is also a position that you can do in Tantric sex.

Kama Sutra Position 3: The Indrani Position

The Indrani position is an excellent position from the Kama Sutra that you can easily introduce into your lovemaking. It is a great position for couples who regularly enjoy the missionary position and is simply a spiced-up version that allows the man to be more in control, with increased physical contact. Both partners will feel the benefits and equally enjoy this position.

How to Perform the Indrani Position

- The man kneels in front of the woman.

- The woman lies on her back with her knees bent up to her chest.

- The woman clasps her hands behind the man's bum and rests her legs by the man's armpits or can push her feet against the man's chest.

Benefits of The Indrani Position

The Indrani is especially good if the man is well endowed. The position itself allows the woman to be more accommodating. It also puts the man in control allowing him to maximize his masculinity. The position is perfect for maximum sensation and arousal. The way the woman's legs are positioned also help to contact vaginal muscles, this will give the woman intense pleasure too, the speed at which the man performs is in his control. Changing speeds during union will build anticipation too, and this will greatly enhance orgasm. The Indrani is brilliant for Tantric sex too.

☐

Kama Sutra Position 4: Milk and Water Embrace

Milk and Water Embrace is great if you are looking to be a bit more adventurous and have sex somewhere other than the bedroom or in your bed. It is easy to do and a great position for beginners.

How to Perform the Milk and Water Embrace

- To do this position, you will need a sturdy chair with no arms.

- The man sits on the chair, and the woman sits on his lap facing away from him.

- To start stroke and arouse each other, the woman can guide the man to her genitals. When fully aroused the man gently raises the woman and enters her. The movement for this position is then to rock back and forth.

Benefits of The Milk and Water Embrace Position

Perfect for beginners and helps explore places to have sexual intercourse away from the bed/bedroom. It is good for foreplay, building anticipation and arousal. The position itself induces powerful orgasms.

☐

Kama Sutra Position 5: The Tigress

As the name suggests, The Tigress makes the woman feel powerful and in control. It is a great turn on for both partners. The Tigress is a very erotic position which is guaranteed to spice things up and ignite passion in your lovemaking. It can take some practice to get used to if the woman is not the usual partner 'on top,' but is worth the practice and will help both partners start to explore new sexual positions.

How to perform the Tigress

- The man lies on the bed on his back.

- The woman sits on top of him with her back to him.

- The woman places one hand on his chest for balance and creating the right position to enable the man to enter her.

- The man then takes hold of the woman's waist and thrust up and down.

Benefits of The Tigress Position

The Tigress is a great confidence giver to the woman. The angle of this pose is very flattering which the man will appreciate, and the woman will feel more confident. A very pleasurable position and a wonderful way to try something different. The Tigress is easy to introduce into your lovemaking.

Kama Sutra Position 6: The Congress of the Crow

The Congress and the Crow is a very raunchy, oral sex position. It does not require much exertion and is easy to perform. It is not a penetrative position but is one that brings close physical contact that allows each partner to pleasure each other at the same time.

How to perform The Congress of the Crow Position

It is like the more common position often referred to as the '69'; The only real difference is that you lie on your side in a fetal position. Each partner gives the other oral stimulation to the genitals.

Benefits of The Congress of the Crow Position

Each partner will receive pleasure at the same time; it is great if you find it hard to orgasm during penetrative sex, it reduces inhibition and is a very erotic position.

Kama Sutra Position 7: The Lotus

Physically, this does need a flexible person, but it can be a great place to start when trying positions from the Kama Sutra for the first time. The position is like the lotus position in yoga.

How to perform The Lotus Position

- The woman lies on her back crossing her legs bringing them up towards her chest.

- The man then pulls the woman close by hooking his legs in.

- The man then thrusts himself in and out of the woman.

Benefits of the Lotus Position

This position is perfect for giving the woman an element of control. It is a very close physical position that allows the man to the woman's breast too. It is particularly good for stimulation of the G-spot.

Kama Sutra Position 8: Suspended Congress

This Suspended Congress is performed standing up, it will require a bit of balance and strength, but after you have mastered this it is one you will want to do again and again!

It is an exciting position and recommended for a passionate sexual union; it will not work so well for a slower, more tantric experience. It can also be performed anywhere as no bed or chair is needed, so is perfect for taking sex outside the bedroom.

How to Perform Suspended Congress

- The man lifts the woman from her bum while the woman grips the man around his waist with her thighs.

- The woman needs to then push her feet against a wall for support.

Benefits of The Suspended Congress

It is a stimulating position and is certain to spice up your sex life. You can do The Suspended Congress anywhere there is a wall or even a tree! It can be very thrilling and will make your pulse race! A great position to try when your sex life needs a bit of a boost.

Kama Sutra Position 9: The Splitting of a Bamboo

The Splitting of a Bamboo may sound painful, but you have probably already tried this or similar without even knowing it! It is a spiced-up version of the missionary position.

How to Perform The Splitting of a Bamboo

- The man lies on top of the woman as in the missionary position.

- The woman raises one leg in the air and rests it on the man's shoulder.

- The woman can change legs during the sexual union.

Benefits of The Splitting of a Bamboo

This position allows for deeper penetration and stimulation for both. It's also a great position to try if you want to become pregnant due to the downward tilt of the woman this position creates.

Kama Sutra Position 10: The Pair of Tongs

The Pair of Tongs is for those with a little more strength and energy. Both partners will need to have good upper body strength, including strong arms.

How to Perform the Pair of Tongs

- The woman lies off the edge of the bed on her side, only the calves, ankle and feet remain on the bed.

- The woman supports herself with her left arm while the man holds her up at the waist.

- The man places his one leg over the woman's left leg holds the woman's right leg up then enters the woman.

Benefits of the Pair of Tongs

An excellent position for inducing strong and intense orgasms. It's also a magnificent work out; it is physically quite demanding. A great position for physically fit and more active and couples.

Kama Sutra Position 11 The Dolphin

To be able to perform the dolphin position you will need a fair bit of strength and flexibility. The Dolphin is for the more advanced.

How to Perform The Dolphin

- The woman lies on the floor and raises her bum, to help do this she will need to press down on the floor firmly with feet.

- The man places himself between her legs and enters her.

- The man then puts his hand beneath the woman's bum and lifts her off the floor.

- The Dolphin is a very physical position which you should not hold for too long.

- Gentle thrusts are required here as harder, faster thrusting can be very uncomfortable and could cause neck injury. Caution is required when practicing this position.

Benefits of the Dolphin

It is perfect for the G-Spot and stimulation

Kama Sutra Position 12: The Curled Angel

The Curled Angel is a spooning position, it is easy to do and is very good for a close, comforting sexual union.

How to Perform the Curled Angel

- Both partners need to lie on their sides, the man spooning the woman.

- She pulls her legs up to her chest which makes penetration from behind very easy.

- The man can either spoon his legs to the woman's or keep them straight or do both.

Benefits of the Curled Angel

It is comforting and romantic position that allows easy penetration which is pleasurable for both.

Kama Sutra Position 13: The Magic Mountain

The Magic Mountain is fun and easy to do. You first need to build a mountain of pillows on the floor. Stack about (3 or 4)

How to Perform the Magic Mountain

She kneels over the pillows with her thighs this pressed together.

He then spoons himself in position kneeling behind her.

The man places his knees on the outside of the woman's legs as he enters. Using his feet to guide penetration and speed.

Benefits of the Magic Mountain

It's easy to do and is a comforting, gentle position. It's great as a slow burner.

Kama Sutra Position 14: The Afternoon Delight

The Afternoon Delight is a beautiful, simple position that is very easy to do.

How to Perform the Afternoon Delight

- The man lies on his side on the bed and props his head up.

- Lying on the bed the women's bottom faces the man's pelvis.

- Sliding toward him the woman places her legs over his body, behind his bottom, she rests her feet on the bed with her feet resting on the bed.

Benefits of the Afternoon Delight

It causes no stress to the body and is also suitable for couples who differ in height. It is an excellent position for those in late pregnancy too.

Kama Sutra Position 15: The Glowing Juniper

The Glowing Juniper is a lovely romantic position and is easy to do.

How to Perform the Glowing Juniper

- The woman lies down and stretches out her legs slightly spreading them.

- The man slides into position, stretching out his legs either side, so his feet are by the woman's ears.

- The man lifts the woman from her waist and enters her.

Benefits of the Glowing Juniper

It's a great position to do with eyes open and is very intimate which promotes bonding and trust.

Conclusion

Practicing techniques and positions from the Tantra and Kama Sutra can significantly improve your sex and love life.

Thank you again for downloading this book!

I hope this book helped you to awaken the real sex god/goddess with- in you.

The next step is to get going!

First try out the bits that you think will work best for you and your partner, then progress on to some of the stuff that takes you out of your comfort zone and see what happens.

Finally, if you enjoyed this book, then I'd like to ask you for a favor, would you be kind enough to leave a review for this book on Amazon? It'd be greatly appreciated!

Thank you and good luck x

CPSIA information can be obtained
at www.ICGtesting.com
Printed in the USA
FSHW022020221120
76212FS